2011
' Twiss for Twissy '
Happy Christmas
Much love
Rita x

TWIGGY
A LIFE IN PHOTOGRAPHS

TWIGGY
A LIFE IN PHOTOGRAPHS

With contributions by
Terence Pepper, Robin Muir
and Melvin Sokolsky

National Portrait Gallery, London

Published in Great Britain by
National Portrait Gallery Publications
National Portrait Gallery
St Martin's Place
London WC2H 0HE

To accompany the display
TWIGGY A Life in Photographs
at the National Portrait Gallery, London
(18 September 2009 – 24 March 2010).

For a complete catalogue of current publications, please
write to the National Portrait Gallery at the address above,
or visit our website at www.npg.org.uk/publications

ISBN 978 1 85514 414 9
A catalogue record for this book is available from
the British Library.

10 9 8 7 6 5 4 3 2 1

Head of Publications: Celia Joicey
Managing Editor: Christopher Tinker
Editor: Tamsin Perrett
Picture Research: Lucy Macmillan
Production: Ruth Müller-Wirth
Design: Studio Dempsey/London
Printed in England by St Ives Westerham Press

Frontispiece: Barry Lategan, 1966
Front cover: Sølve Sundsbø, 2009
Back cover: Melvin Sokolsky, 1967

CONTENTS

INTRODUCTION

As fashion model and photographic muse to many of the world's most significant photographers, Twiggy personified the particular 'London Look' that forever defined the late 1960s. Aged only sixteen, freckle-faced, five foot six and weighing just six and a half stone, Twiggy – born sixty years ago this September – was an unlikely candidate to become the world's first supermodel. This she achieved in a modelling career that ran initially from early 1966 to the end of the decade – just four years – at a feverish pitch and as the subject of continuous press fascination.

From the outset Twiggy collaborated with the leading photographers of the time. She was launched with a full-page profile by fashion writer Deirdre McSharry in the *Daily Express*, which published pictures by Barry Lategan. He also took the first fashion shots of Twiggy for the *Daily Sketch*, then a best-selling newspaper.

At school Twiggy had shared the cost of buying *Vogue* with her friends. Suddenly she was featured in the magazine, which shared the spotlight – with *Queen* and *Elle* – as the most prestigious fashion publication. Twiggy worked with Cecil Beaton, Helmut Newton, Norman Parkinson, Ronald Traeger and Guy Bourdin. She also worked with Terry O'Neill and David Steen, who first established their reputations as press and reportage photographers. In America Twiggy sat for Francesco Scavullo.

She posed for extended narrative images with *Harper's Bazaar* photographer Melvin Sokolsky and for American *Vogue* with Bert Stern, who would also make two documentaries for CBS Television of Twiggy's first arrival in New York and a thirty-minute programme covering her trip to Hollywood.

Twiggy's early stated ambition had been to work with Richard Avedon, the most highly rated fashion photographer of the era, and the results of their collaboration were quickly recognized as some of the most iconic fashion studies of the decade. Two of these photographs appear in The Metropolitan Museum of Art's recent publication *The Model as Muse* (Yale, 2009) and the image of Twiggy in a backless, striped silver dress appeared on both the poster and the invitation to American *Vogue*'s Met Ball in New York in May 2009.

By the end of the 1960s there were few heights left for her to scale as a fashion model, and Twiggy had also achieved huge export success with her own range of clothes. She began her career in theatre, music and dance with two Golden Globe awards for her starring role in Ken Russell's film *The Boy Friend* (1971). The portrait by Douglas Kirkland of Twiggy at that time shows the change from ex-Mod queen to a maturing woman. Twiggy has made several films, recorded chart hits and albums, gaining a silver disc and famously starring on Broadway in New York in the Tony award-winning musical *My One and Only* (1983–4).

Whilst working on a concurrent National Portrait Gallery project on 1960s' pop music, 'Beatles to Bowie: The 60s Exposed', we decided to look at Twiggy's extraordinary rise to worldwide fame. That this moment coincides with Twiggy's own sixtieth birthday and a new, exciting phase of her modelling career made this idea of a complementary celebration highly attractive.

I was pleasantly surprised to find how many times Twiggy had already been on the walls of the National Portrait Gallery before this more studied examination of her iconography, which we make as part of our mission to record history through portraiture. The Gallery's first-ever photography exhibition, a Cecil Beaton retrospective in 1968, included an image of Twiggy that is shown again here. 'A Masque of Beauty' (1972), a look at beauties through the centuries, had a blue-toned print of Twiggy by Barry Lategan, shown in the chronology of this publication on the cover of London *Look* (1967).

Twiggy was shown in 1981 as part of Norman Parkinson's first retrospective, 'Fifty Years of Portraits and Fashion', and eight years later images from her first shoot for a glossy magazine were included in Lewis Morley's retrospective, 'Photographer of the Sixties' (1989). For Richard Avedon's 1995 retrospective a huge enlargement of Twiggy's four seasons shoot (also published here) was chosen to hang by the entrance, and the exhibition provided the opportunity for photographer and muse to meet again. In the twenty-first century Twiggy's appearances at the Gallery have become even more frequent. In 2003 she featured in 'Lichfield: The Early Years', as part of an 'In Crowd' captured for *Queen* magazine. Also that year she was in 'British Blondes' (a study by Allan Ballard) and Terry O'Neill's retrospective 'Celebrity' (Twiggy at the start of her career, with her mother). Twiggy standing on a pedestal, in an orange dress designed by John Bates, was a highlight of the Gallery's 2004 exhibition 'Beaton: Portraits', still touring in part in 2009. And most recently of all a pregnant Twiggy was the covergirl for our display of Bernard Schwartz's 1970s portraits.

In 1993 Twiggy returned to modelling with a dramatic portfolio shot by Steven Meisel for Italian *Vogue*, and she has since worked with photographers ranging from Brian Aris, Annie Leibovitz, Bryan Adams and Mary McCartney to Sølve Sundsbø, who photographed her for the cover of the cutting-edge fashion magazine *i-D*. With Twiggy's very active and insightful collaboration, we hope this book will inform and entertain, and reflect the well-deserved and special place she holds as an icon of our times.

Terence Pepper
Curator of Photographs,
National Portrait Gallery, London

SUPER NEW THING: TWIGGY, VOGUE AND THE YOUNG IDEA

Within minutes of touching down at John F. Kennedy airport, New York, on a Monday afternoon in late March 1967, the model Twiggy found herself caught up in a churning mass of photographers, journalists, fans and bystanders. At seventeen, London's hottest property had arrived and was something of a curiosity. Fashion and 'Pop' culture had collided to produce a new kind of woman who looked nothing like a woman usually looked. Her blonde hair had been cut short into a signature boyish crop, her five-foot-six frame was angular to the point of wonderment, her breasts were barely perceptible, and her wide-eyed expression was reinforced by three rows of false lashes. Her demeanour was startling for its lack of conceit and unexpected for its naturalness and, to round it off, she spoke in an accent that many Americans found impenetrable when she was exuberant, which was most of the time.

In less than a year Twiggy – born Lesley Hornby in Neasden, north London – had become a global phenomenon. She was by far the most internationally recognizable model, and the embodiment of the fashion world's 'Young Idea' in Britain and 'Youthquake' in America. *Vogue* explained the persona: 'Twiggy is called Twiggy because she looks as if a strong gale would snap her in two and dash her to the ground. In a profession where thinness is essential, Twiggy is of such a meagre constitution that other models stare at her' – but the magazine was at a loss to explain her transcendency.[1] She was newsworthy not solely for her remarkable looks, but because her new-found fame and the speed with which she had achieved it had become as much the story to report. *Vogue* deduced that the public's appetite for novelty was becoming a phenomenon in itself: voracious, insatiable and likely to be fleeting.

'Twiggy – the willowy shoot of seventeen who has just sprouted under the camera's hot lights.'[2] In identifying the new model by name early on, American *Vogue* did much to ensure that her celebrity grew in tandem with her modelling career. Her fame also made sense to those caught up in the era's well-documented clash of cultures. 'Today's look comes from below. The working class girl with money in her pocket can be as chic as the deb. That's what Twiggy is all about.'[3] Always in tune to the pulse-beat of fashionable life, Cecil Beaton's aperçu was acutely observed.

Twiggy's manager, 'Justin de Villeneuve' (properly Nigel Davies from Edmonton, north-east London), had joined her on that first flight to New York. The former boxer, bookie's clerk and hairstylist explained her away to America as a 'sort of mini-Queen of the new social aristocracy.'[4] With daily access to Twiggy during her first weeks in America, Thomas Whiteside of the *New Yorker* witnessed at first hand the 'observable fact' of Twiggy as a 'Super New Thing'.[5] Trailed by photographer and film-maker Bert Stern for a series of documentaries, Twiggy's every utterance and gesture was recorded, to the extent that Whiteside could claim with a degree of horror: '[She] was completely plugged in, aurally and visually, becoming almost literally an extension of the cameras – ninety-one pounds of human feedback.'[6]

Twiggy's life had already changed by 1967. *Life* magazine had made two separate features out of her heart-stopping rise from Saturday girl at a Neasden hairdresser's to the country's most famous fashion model.[7] A cover story in *Newsweek* went into hyperbolic overdrive: 'She is the magic child of the media … an adolescent angel … Nothing like her has happened since the Beatles.'[8] She was Britain's 'Face of '66', and before she left for six weeks in New York had appeared in thirteen separate fashion shoots for *Vogue* – British, French and American – then, as now, the high point of a modelling career.

Vogue's standards of excellence were unrivalled, and within its pages Twiggy would stand or run or jump or do anything at all, with the exception of taking off her clothes, for fashion photography's greatest names: Guy Bourdin (though only her legs appeared in the final pictures);[9] Helmut Newton (for whom she wore a silver 'Space Race' mini-dress);[10] and Norman Parkinson (for whom she swung on a rope). For her first *Vogue* shoot, taken in February 1966, she had stood in a muddy field for David Montgomery.[11] Her latest *Vogue* pictures, 'Spring Action!' by Helmut Newton, already on the magazine racks as she left London, showed the newcomer at her most dynamic.[12]

Photographed for *Vogue* but not yet released were another two sets by Newton; three by the up-and-coming Frenchman Just Jaeckin (one of which was considered too experimental and subsequently scrapped);[13] a cover and eight editorial pages for French *Vogue* by the courtly American Henry Clarke;[14] and a 'Paris Collections' feature photographed by Bert Stern for American *Vogue* and shared with French *Vogue*, 'Twiggy: Haute Couture', becoming 'Twiggy: Le Mannequin-Vedette 1967' a month later.[15] There was the still-to-come *plein air* series by Ronald Traeger, a rising star, and the Frenchman Jeanloup Sieff.[16] Then there was the never-to-appear: Bob Richardson, *Vogue*'s maverick genius, photographed the phenomenon but his pictures, now lost, were never used.[17]

But here in New York, amid the sweeping, jostling, frantic scramble that took Twiggy from plane to press conference, 'in a series of sharp flashes like heat lightning' as one onlooker put it, was the evidence that whatever changes fame and photography had wrought so far, in New York her life would change irrevocably.[18] Press attention and 'the click of hurrying heels, the slapping of soles and the tripping of amateur camera shutters' would be almost ceaseless, the *New Yorker* predicted.[19] It proved by its own example that this would be the case. 'A Super New Thing', stretched out over nearly 100 pages, was the longest the magazine had yet run on a popular cultural topic.

Twiggy was 'the Superstar Model' as *Vogue* put it, 'the master pattern for a million teenagers all over the world. A heroine for her time, which is now.'[20] However, on meeting her at the airport, her modelling agent, Barbara Thorbahn, admitted with alacrity that 'really she's not a model at this time. She's a celebrity.'[21] Already working outside the accepted system, magazines were nonplussed by Twiggy's lack of pushiness and the fact that at seventeen she was the consummate professional, betraying neither ennui nor exhaustion. The writer Polly Devlin suggested that this was only possible because she could 'remain the centre of her own world by not seeing those who don't enter it'.[22] Some observers went even further. As early as February 1966, Robin Douglas-Home in the *Daily Express*, the newspaper that had launched Twiggy as 'The Face of 1966', remarked: 'Isn't it about time someone finally punctured this idiotic, currently fashionable balloon of hero-worshipping fashion photographers and models and of treating them as some sort of gods and goddesses flown in from outer space to become contemporary idols ....'[23]

The media theorist Marshall McLuhan sought to make sense of it all: 'Her power is incompleteness … Any person with a very undefined, casual, spontaneous image requires the viewer to complete it.'[24] That she could be anything anyone wanted her to be, which was perhaps McLuhan's point, was summed up more directly by the beauty editor of *Seventeen*: 'I found her fantastic! It's like watching poetry. She's Harlow, she's Garbo. She's all kinds of people ....'[25] She was

a brand and a fashion entity, and by 1967 she was a toy doll too. She had her own magazine, *Twiggy*, a fashion line, cosmetic endorsements, 'Twiggy Stix' eyeliners and eyelashes, and, curiously, board games and lunch-boxes. All were controlled through the London-based Twiggy Enterprises.

The noise resounded across the Atlantic well before she arrived. Watching the phenomenon unfold, Twiggy's American photographers worked elements of her burgeoning fame into their own photographs. Bert Stern's 'Paris Collections' series for American and French *Vogues* made a direct allusion to the media furore surrounding the teenage sensation. The most intriguing showed Twiggy in isolation, staring back at her face reflected in several television monitors dotted around the studio. That her face appeared lost and vulnerable beneath the striations of the screen made the photographs more troubling. 'Who knows what drama lurks off-stage?' ran one caption.[26] Twiggy's celebrity had placed her under intense scrutiny and shortly after her arrival Melvin Sokolsky amplified this in a surreal set of photographs that put her identity under even closer examination. In the most arresting frame his subject is all but overpowered by passers-by wielding black-and-white 'Twiggy' masks. It was now an unavoidable consequence of any location shoot with Twiggy that a crowd would gather, and Sokolsky made a virtue out of it. Massing the onlookers around her – 'ordinary' people, despite the disquieting masks – Twiggy faced a barrier, almost invisible, a plate glass shop window, through which Sokolsky made his photograph. Reflecting the frenzy of her arrival in New York, he raised Stern's implications of voyeurism and scrutiny in the Twiggy phenomenon to a level of concern. Her popularity was unsettling and there was, by Sokolsky's reckoning, nowhere to run. 'I felt I was from outer space,' Twiggy would write later.'[27] She was already identifiable as a celebrity/model, and now Sokolsky defined her as something approaching a commodity.

The opportunity offered by American *Vogue* to work with Richard Avedon, its star photographer, was one of the reasons New York held allure. Avedon was the type of fashion photographer people had in mind whenever they thought of a fashion photographer: gregarious, charming, unmoved by hemline debates, but focused entirely on the girl and the picture. He was articulate too, and cerebral, and his imprimatur could propel a model girl into the pantheon. *Newsweek*'s verdict had already been dispiriting: 'four straight limbs in search of a woman's body',[28] and among Twiggy's first words to America was the now-folkloric, 'Well, it's not what you'd call a *figure*, is it?'[29] Avedon may have embraced the statuesque Veruschka von Lehndorff as muse and found inspiration in the coltish Jean Shrimpton, Twiggy's heroine whilst a teenager, but he had asked for Twiggy, and the signs were good: 'I'm interested in young girls not because of knock knees and tongues sticking out but because of what I can find about them that is beautiful. With Twiggy, I consider the

shape of her head beautiful, and also the simplicity and gentleness of her gestures; even the narrowness of her leg is interesting.'[30]

Avedon did not disappoint. 'He makes you *feel* beautiful,' Twiggy wrote, qualifying it years later: 'He made me look like a woman.'[31] Avedon regarded Twiggy as unspoilt by experience and entirely malleable: 'The less she did, the truer the pictures seemed to be – truer to herself, truer to my work.' He also recognized her uniqueness: 'I think what's involved is the stripping away of certain affectations about what is beautiful. Twiggy is made for that.'[32]

Between July 1967 and April 1968, *Vogue* published forty-eight pictures of Twiggy by Avedon alone. He would later photograph her as the four seasons for *McCalls* magazine. Bert Stern also would undertake some final sessions with Twiggy for *Vogue*.

In Britain too her star showed little sign of waning. Casting her as a *fin de siècle* dandy, Helmut Newton emphasized her androgyny, while Cecil Beaton, enjoying a career renaissance in his sixties, cast her as a 'cosmic Ariel' dancing around his Kensington home, standing on a marble plinth and swinging her legs from the top of a cupboard.[33] Beaton was, *prima facie*, charmed: 'She is an easy little marvel of photo-graphy. Can't look wrong.'[34] Later, in *Vogue* he wrote, more puzzled by than disdainful of, her 'concave droop as of a punctured marionette'.[35] In a similar vein, Diana Vreeland, editor-in-chief of American *Vogue* and the brilliant orchestrator of Twiggy's success with Avedon, stated publicly that 'She's delicious looking.'[36] 'We love her silky throat, her naturalness, her inner serenity,'[37] she declared, while admonishing Avedon privately on the mechanics necessary to achieve naturalness and serenity: '… handle her as a precious package … ask her to pull in her behind and shoot up her spine and you'll have the glorious girl … sullen eyes and pouting lips should not appear in [American] *Vogue*.'[38]

In 1970, at the age of twenty, Twiggy retired from modelling (although she would concede the occasional shoot for *Vogue*). She had modelled for four and a half years as 'an affront to femininity' or 'the most radiant and evocative new image', depending on whom you believed.[39] Her status as a fashion icon was assured. Richard Avedon's dynamic series is now regarded as a masterpiece of fashion photography.

Twiggy became a star of stage and screen, most notably – and shimmeringly – in Ken Russell's film musical *The Boy Friend* (1971), for which she won two Golden Globe awards. A respectable Broadway career began with *My One and Only* (1983–4). Her fame, especially in America, far outlived a fashion for triple-layered false lashes and a range of stick-thin dolls, and the transition to acting and dancing seemed effortless. 'I didn't plan to do anything. I didn't plan to be a model. I didn't plan to be a singer. I didn't plan to be an actress.'[40]

She returned to modelling in 1993 at the request of Italian *Vogue* and the American photographer Steven Meisel, whom she considered 'the Avedon of the Nineties'. A keen student of fashion photography, Meisel had observed Avedon's modus operandi and reinterpreted it in the modern idiom, specifically, the slow shutter-speed 'jump' technique that Avedon had himself reworked from the pre-war photographs of Martin Munkacsi.

Meisel's portfolio, extending over seventeen pages, was a resounding success, and Italian *Vogue*, available on import in limited numbers, sold out its run in Britain.[41] Twiggy then sat, after nearly twenty years away from the fashion pages, for several magazines, notably *Tatler*, who reunited her with Barry Lategan, whose photographs from 1966 had first propelled her into the public eye.[42] As the twenty-first century approached, *Vogue* glanced back to its heritage for 'Millennium' special issues, and Twiggy featured in new photographs by Nick Knight (for British *Vogue*) and Annie Leibovitz (for American *Vogue*).[43] Her status was assured and allowed her to move forward in the world of fashion. Her own valediction to an extraordinary moment in fashion photographic history and the 'Twiggy' phenomenon is stark but characteristically self-effacing: 'I used to be a thing,' she said. 'I'm a person now.'

Robin Muir

Notes on page 141

TWIGGY: A DIFFERENT RHYTHM

New York City, March 1967. The front door opened and Twiggy entered the studio with her small entourage. I observed her from a distance as my assistant led her through a myriad set pieces to meet me. It took no more than a few steps for me to notice that Twiggy moved to a different rhythm from that of anyone I had ever seen. She at once revealed a charming persona and wit that were instantly engaging. I was intrigued to realize that she was only seventeen years old.

Although Twiggy weighed no more than ninety pounds, she was not as painfully thin and lacking in femininity as had been reported. She reminded me of the woman in the Hans Memling painting of Eve, *sans* the tummy. Physically, she was obviously of a more modern genotype, with small but feminine breasts. Twiggy loved clothes and wore them rather than the clothes wearing her. My intuition urged me to give her unrestricted freedom so that I could explore her unorthodox gift of body language in order to present her at her best. A simple gesture such as a raised shoulder said it all.

I was astonished by her seemingly overnight meteoric rise to fame. This phenomenon triggered the idea of photographing her in various situations in which passers-by and cast members would be photographed wearing 'Twiggy' masks. The theme was: 'Everyone Wants to Be Twiggy'. I shot various portraits of Twiggy a few days before the shoot that were cut out and made into face-masks. The masks were handed out to passers-by at each of the chosen locations. Hundreds of people lined up, literally begging to be in the pictures.

It was Twiggy's unaffected presence that translated into an inimitable body language and it was this that captivated her fans. It convinced us all that this teenager was the metaphor for a new era of how women would be perceived and respected for their individuality.

Melvin Sokolsky

MY LIFE IN PHOTOGRAPHS

Over the past forty years I have been privileged to work with some of the most talented and amazing photographers in the world.

When I was about fourteen I had a bedroom wall covered with pictures of my favourite models Jean Shrimpton and Jane Birkin, among others. I was already obsessed with fashion and making my own clothes. Little did I dream that within a couple of years I would be following in their footsteps – travelling the world and working with these brilliant photographers.

This book is a collection of photographs, both professional and private, from throughout my career, and my memories of how, when and where they were taken. Who knew that some of those original photographs would now grace the walls of the National Portrait Gallery and be the subject of a book – it's all very thrilling.

THE PROCESS

Having been in the photographic industry – albeit on the other side of the camera – since the 1960s, it's been fascinating for me to see how the process has changed. When I first started modelling everything was shot on film and you saw nothing until the film had been processed – taking a few days – then from the contact sheet you would choose the shot and send it off again to the printer to await the final print. And retouching was a fine art done by hand, by very talented people who would scratch and paint out the unwanted blemishes on the actual print.

Now, of course, with digital cameras everything is instant. I remember the first time I worked digitally not liking it, as everyone – except me – was huddled round the computer, rearranging, adjusting and picking or rejecting shots as they went along. I felt it would interfere with that special rapport and trust between the photographer and model. But it hasn't, and I quite like that immediate element now. Although there was always a great excitement and anticipation in the waiting, I'm surprised to find I don't miss it at all.

What's fascinating to me about working with so many different, brilliant photographers is seeing the results of our collaboration on each shoot. It's the same me, but I'm constantly amazed at which particular aspects of my personality – and theirs – they choose to reveal.

BARRY LATEGAN

Let's start at the beginning: 1966. I was sixteen – a shy, skinny schoolgirl, a Mod. Mad about fashion and making clothes. My plan was to get into art school, study design and become a dress designer. An older friend who worked on a ladies' magazine suggested I try modelling and arranged for a meeting with her fashion editor. Nervously, but excitedly, I went to the meeting. I was gutted when she told me that at five foot six and a half I was too small to be a fashion model. But she also said I had an interesting face and could maybe do head shots. She sent me off to get my hair done for some test shots.

The hairdresser was the House of Leonard, a posh Mayfair townhouse off Grosvenor Square. I was very intimidated – I'd never been anywhere so grand. While I was having my shoulder-length hair styled, a lovely man came over and asked my name. He was Leonard, the famous hairdresser and owner of the salon.

Unbeknownst to me, he then called Barry Lategan, a young, very talented photographer, to say he had a girl in the salon on whom he'd like to try out his new crop haircut. Leonard arranged for me to go to Barry's so he could see if I was photogenic.

Apparently Barry thought so. He was so sweet to me that day. When he asked my name and was told it was Twiggy (my nickname) he said if I ever did model, I should use it.

A few days later, a day off school, I spent about seven hours having my hair coloured by Daniel Galvin and cut by Leonard into that little-boyish crop that was to become famous. The next day Barry took a series of head shots for Leonard to show his new cut. It was my first professional time in front of a camera: I remember being very nervous and not really knowing what to do. But I was extremely lucky that my first session was with dear Barry. Not only is he a wonderful photographer, but he handled me with kid gloves and was kind and funny, and he got some wonderful photographs.

Leonard hung one of the shots in the lobby of his salon and I went back to school, amazing my friends with my new look. That really could have been that, but for the fact that one of Leonard's clients was Deirdre McSharry, fashion editor on the *Daily Express* and a very influential lady in the fashion world. When she saw the photo – she loved the haircut – she enquired who the model was. Leonard told her it was a young schoolgirl called Twiggy and she went about arranging an interview with me for her paper. So, taking yet another day off school, I went up to Fleet Street to the *Daily Express* offices and had tea with Deirdre. They took more pictures of me and she asked me about my life and my dreams.

Having been told by her that she would write a piece about me, my dear dad would get the *Express* every day. For about three weeks nothing appeared, then one morning Dad came into my bedroom with an open newspaper and excitedly showed me the article. It covered almost the whole page. Deirdre announced 'Twiggy – the Face of '66'. Well, at that moment my life changed for ever.

I now realize the importance of the relationship with the person behind the camera. Barry made that shy little girl believe that the lens was her friend and taught her just to be natural, to work with the lens.

So I have a lot to thank Barry Lategan for – as I do with all of the photographers appearing in this book.

ALLAN BALLARD

Allan Ballard was one of a group of four young photographers who worked for the short-lived and very hip *London Life* magazine, which was the first magazine to publish a photograph of me in their street fashion series 'What People Are Wearing'. He had previously worked for four years for the top fashion photographer John Cowan, whose studio was later used in Antonioni's film *Blow-Up* (1966).

We worked together for a special feature that the *Daily Sketch* set up, covering Paris fashion week at the end of January 1967. I visited the major shows with Shirley Flack, the fashion editor, and the paper carried a daily account of our impressions of each show, together with a photograph by Allan showing me previewing a new creation. The image we have chosen shows me in an ensemble created by Jacques Esterel, who was then best known as a designer for Brigitte Bardot.

Several years later I worked with Allan again when he took a series of pictures of me rehearsing for a short British tour in 1977 to promote my new album, including venues such as Brighton and the Royal Albert Hall. We used several of the pictures, including the one showing me posing on a chair, in the official tour programme.

DAVID STEEN

As well as working with me on fashion shoots, David Steen also took photographs of me for my first autobiography in 1968 (rather prematurely published when I was eighteen years old). His wife, journalist Shirley Flack, who I'd worked with in Paris, was helping me write the book, so I would spend long weekends at their gorgeous house in Surrey. They made me feel like one of the family, and I have many happy memories of our time spent together. Because I got to know David, Shirley and the family so well, David took some wonderful reportage photographs that captured the non-modelling moments.

I worked with David later, in the 1970s, when he did some wonderful portraits of me as Eliza Doolittle in a TV production of *Pygmalion*.

BERT STERN

In 1967 the legendary Diana Vreeland – editor-in-chief of American *Vogue*, the most powerful woman in fashion – booked me to do my first spread for the magazine. Bert Stern took the photographs, which were of the Paris collections. The photograph of me sitting on a monitor, with the screen simultaneously showing my face being filmed, was part of this shoot. Halfway through the shoot, which took place over about a week, I managed to sprain my ankle badly. So I turned up at the studio with my foot and lower leg heavily bandaged. In a flash of inspiration, Bert worked out he could shoot me with my damaged foot cleverly hidden behind various objects.

Bert is also a film-maker. He had directed the famous documentary *Jazz on a Summer's Day*, a film about the Newport Jazz Festival for which he won numerous accolades and awards. On my first visit to New York, later in 1967, Bert was asked by CBS Television to do a documentary on my visit. So we had lots of happy times together, and it's wonderful for me to have his film as a memory of that time. Bert also shot me for the cover of *Newsweek* magazine on that trip.

MELVIN SOKOLSKY

At the same time as doing the CBS documentary with Bert Stern, I was shooting an ad campaign with Mel Sokolsky. My memories of working with him are of an extraordinary experience at an extraordinary time. It was my first trip to New York in 1967. He was a modern, 'hot' photographer. He stretched the boundaries in fashion photography. His 1963 photograph for *Harper's Bazaar* of girls in clear bubbles floating above the set is one of the most famous from that time. For the big ad campaign he came up with the idea of a story showing me at famous landmarks around New York – the Statue of Liberty, Staten Island Ferry, Broadway – taking part in a ticker-tape parade, and outside a large department store. On the first day of the shoot a problem arose because onlookers kept getting in the frame, so Mel came up with the idea of making masks from black-and-white photographs of my face, which he gave to the crowd to wear.

It worked amazingly well and the images became very famous. Melvin and the art direction team won several awards. It was a great success … although I nearly got crushed on one occasion because the crowd outside the department store location started to really grow and people pushed in from all around. I got pretty hysterical. Luckily, Melvin had hired a bodyguard friend and former Mr Universe, Harold, to protect me. It's useful to have a Mr Universe in your life on such occasions. I remember Harold's upper arm was the same measurement as my waist! He scooped me up under his arm, ran through the crowd, and gently hoisted me through the open back window of the waiting limousine, where I lay sobbing on the floor.

RICHARD AVEDON

Avedon was undoubtedly the master of his craft. He changed the face of fashion photography in the 1940s and '50s. Rather than shooting static, almost emotionless models, he had his subjects show real emotions – laughing, smiling, leaping, dancing. His fame began as chief photographer for *Harper's Bazaar*, but in 1966 he switched camps to work for American *Vogue* under the stewardship of its brilliant editor–in–chief, Diana Vreeland. So when Vreeland brought me to New York in 1967 she booked me with Richard Avedon. At that time being photographed by Avedon was the goal for most models, so I felt totally overwhelmed to be working with him so soon. I was barely seventeen and still pretty shy. A shoot with Dick was an extraordinary experience. He was a petite, pixie-like, intense man with a mass of thick black hair, and thick, black-rimmed glasses. Over the next few years I did a few sessions with Dick and the results were always a bit special.

One time in New York, Dick was shooting me with a very precious diamond glued to my forehead. It was absolutely huge and God knows what it was worth. I was amazed there were no big bodyguards around guarding the goods (not me, the diamond). Then Dick pointed out a little elderly lady sitting in the corner of the studio, complete with granny glasses, felt hat and small, brown handbag … in which was a silver Smith & Wesson revolver. She was the guard – much less obvious than you would expect – brilliant! The photo came out pretty well too.

I'm particularly fond of the portraits Dick did of me as the four seasons. They were black-and-white photographs that were then hand-coloured, a technique he had used on his portraits of the Beatles in 1967. The extraordinary thing about my seasons pictures is how he 'matures' the image from spring to winter, not with make-up and lines, but with his lighting and the way he captures my emotions. The autumn shot with my fake hair is probably the most famous of the series. In 1995, when I was invited to the opening of Avedon's exhibition at the National Portrait Gallery, I was so thrilled that he chose to blow up the shot and it was the first photo you saw as

you entered the exhibition. It was a wonderful night altogether. Number one, to meet up with Dick again after over twenty-five years, and also to meet Princess Diana, who opened the exhibition. I had the privilege of a private tour through the exhibition with her, Dick explaining the shots. It's a very precious memory for me. Diana later wrote me a sweet letter that I cherish.

For nearly forty years I carried in my Filofax a small contact photo of Dick and me leaping through the air (taken by his assistant) – but it was falling to pieces. When I was working as a judge on *America's Next Top Model*, the photographer on the set offered to get a copy made of it, to preserve the image reproduced here. For me, it somehow crosses the barriers between the professional and the personal. I treasure it and feel very fortunate to have worked with this extremely talented artist.

FRANCESCO SCAVULLO

For a time Francesco's photography seemed to dominate the fashion world. He was a huge influence on American fashion and his photographs featured on the covers of *Rolling Stone*, *Life*, *Time*, *Harper's Bazaar*, *Vogue* and *Queen*. Most famously, he shot the covers of *Cosmopolitan* for thirty years, as well as many movie posters.

He produced some beautiful images, portraits and still lifes. His work includes portraits of Gloria Vanderbilt, Grace Kelly, Elizabeth Taylor, Paul Newman and Joanna Woodward, Diana Ross, Cher, Brad Pitt, Brooke Shields, Madonna and Andy Warhol.

Francesco was a lovely man and I enjoyed working with him. I only realized while doing this book that on both shoots – fifteen years apart – I'm wearing a hat. A red hat. He obviously saw me as a red hat gal. I'm glad about that – I've always loved hats. I was surprised and delighted to be invited to the second shoot we're including in this book, which was for a portolio of America's most beautiful women.

I'm glad I knew and worked with Francesco. He knew how to make women look beautiful. 'I'm impressed by glamour,' he told an interviewer. 'I'm impressed by beauty. I'm impressed by charming people. I'm impressed! I'm impressed!'

JEANLOUP SIEFF

Jeanloup Sieff was one of the great names in fashion photography when we worked together in the 1960s. He was best known for his high-fashion work for magazines such as *Harper's Bazaar*, *Vogue*, *Glamour* and *Esquire*. Dancers and nudes were recurring themes in his work. I didn't do the nude bits, but I do love the shots he took of me in the woods just outside Paris. They have a haunting quality – I was young and inexperienced, but he created an atmosphere I could work in. He was very encouraging and lovely to work with.

RONALD TRAEGER

Ronald Traeger was taken from us far too early – at the age of only thirty-two. When we met in the mid 1960s he was a young photographer, painter and graphic designer.

We worked together a lot in my early career, and there's no doubt Traeger would have gone on producing wonderful pictures, pushing the boundaries and experimenting. He captured the era of 'Swinging London'. His photographs have a wonderful spirit about them. The shot of me on a bicycle, laughing, has been reproduced in postcard and poster form and I still see it all over the world. Traeger mostly photographed me outside on location, and I have happy memories of running up and down the Kings Road in Chelsea and him following me with a camera.

CECIL BEATON

In the 1940s and '50s Cecil Beaton was known as the Queen's photographer. No, not *Queen* magazine, Queen Elizabeth the Queen Mother. In fact I think he photographed most of the Royal Family at the time. His photographs have a regal, timeless quality. He was also a huge influence as a dress designer and won two Academy Awards: for his costume design for the film *Gigi* and art direction on *My Fair Lady*.

In 1972 Beaton was knighted for his contribution to the arts.

When I got the offer to work with him in the late 1960s I was thrilled. His work was incredibly stylish and his photographs somehow reflected the passing of an age. Although I was the face and look of a new generation, ironically I always had a penchant for the 1920s, '30s and '40s – that's where my heart was. I loved the clothes, the music, the movies. Still do. In fact my all-time hero is Fred Astaire – he completely epitomizes the glamour of that era for me.

As I was used to being a cute teenager in most shoots, I was very excited at the prospect of doing a more sophisticated session with Cecil. Sadly for me that wasn't to be. I think he wanted to be very modern, so the shoot proceeded with me in little mini-dresses, sitting and standing on various pieces of furniture – even on top of a wardrobe – and most famously in a yellow velvet dress on top of a Roman pillar. I remember him being very polite and seeming very old – but I was a teenager and anyone over the age of twenty-five was ancient. I was a little intimidated, but he was extremely kind to me. I'm very honoured to have worked with this great man.

KLAUS VOORMANN

As well as the hard work, getting up for a shoot at 7a.m. for an often eleven- or twelve-hour day, a lot of the fun of those times was meeting some of the people I did. One of them was German-born Klaus Voormann. He is probably best known as the bass guitarist in the British band Manfred Mann. He was living in London in the 1960s – we met and became friends. As well as being a fantastic musician, he is also the most wonderful artist – most famously, at that time, for designing the Beatles' *Revolver* cover. His artwork is superb. His work on a set of fashion photographs taken by Justin de Villeneuve is remarkable. He was given black-and-white prints that he would transform into works of art. I adore the one we've featured in which I appear to be running and the perspective and flowing hair he added to the photograph takes it into another, surreal realm. Klaus is a lovely man and a true artist. We still keep in touch.

LINDA McCARTNEY

In the late 1960s I got a call from my friend Paul McCartney. His new American girlfriend Linda was coming to live in London. He was concerned that she didn't have any female friends over here and asked if I'd get together with her. We met for lunch at San Lorenzo restaurant. We hit it off immediately and there began a thirty-year friendship. I have so many wonderful memories of Linda. She was a fantastic friend, a wonderful wife and mother, and also an incredibly talented photographer.

I never actually sat for Linda. That wasn't the way she worked. She always had a camera with her, so, as in the tradition of all great reportage photographers, she would capture wonderful moments. It was just natural for her to snap away. At home. In the garden. In the studio. On the beach. At the table. She was one of the best, as a woman, as a friend and as a photographer.

I love the picture of me in a woolly hat: it brings back memories of many happy times together. Linda featured it in her book of photographs of the 1960s. A week after their daughter Mary was born, in August 1969, I went over to see her and Linda took this picture in the glasshouse at the bottom of their garden.

DOUGLAS KIRKLAND

At the age of twenty-four, Canadian-born Douglas Kirkland was hired as a staff photographer for *Look* magazine in the USA. He became famous for his 1961 photospread of Marilyn Monroe, which was taken for the magazine's twenty-fifth anniversary. Dougie photographed me for *Look* magazine in 1970. They were interested in how I was developing in my new career, so the session was about me as a woman, not a fashion shoot. The shots were done at my home and consequently had a spontaneity about them.

Dougie also photographed me on the set of *The Boy Friend* – my first film – in 1970.

NORMAN PARKINSON

I'm so glad I had the chance to work with Norman Parkinson. We did a shoot together once during the 1960s, but the shots I like best were taken in the late 1970s – especially the one of me pregnant with my daughter Carly. He chose to do the shot quite sparsely, by an attic window with an umbilical-like electric cord on the floor. It's probably one of my favourite pictures. He was quite elderly when our paths crossed, but he was delightful. Completely eccentric, he was very tall and thin with a large moustache and he always wore a beautiful embroidered Kashmiri wedding hat and very hippyish clothes, which I loved. He was in every way unique.

TERRY O'NEILL

Terry is always a joy to work with. Having spent a lot of his career photographing huge stars on film sets, he is very in control and comfortable in what he is doing on a shoot. The first time we had an assigment together was in 1966 just after the 'Face of '66' piece in the *Daily Express*. He came over to get shots of me and my mum and dad at home. This being the mid-1960s, he had shoulder-length blond hair. He was also very handsome. When he rang the doorbell my mum took one look at his face and said, 'Come in, miss!' She really thought he was a girl. We laughed so much, and still do.

Terry has captured important moments in my life over the years: during the 1970s when I was recording my first albums; in the 1990s; and then in 2008 when he photographed my daughter Carly and me for *Marie Claire* magazine. From being a huge bump in my womb in the Norman Parkinson pictures, my then twenty-nine-year-old daughter was being photographed with me by Terry O'Neill. Another circle completed.

STEVEN MEISEL

It was Steven who persuaded me back into modelling in 1993. I'd been a fan of his work for a long time. He called and asked if I would sit for him for the cover of Italian *Vogue* and ten pages inside. I was truly flattered and couldn't refuse. Steven is undoubtedly one of the great fashion photographers. His campaigns for Versace, Valentino, Dolce & Gabbana, Calvin Klein and Prada are legendary.

I arrived at his studio in New York and started doing my hair and make-up. Steven arrived about an hour later and I said hello and how thrilled I was to meet him. He then told me we'd met before. I was slightly embarrassed – I didn't remember – but he said there was no way I would as he was twelve years old at the time!

Back in 1967, when I was working with Melvin Sokolsky, Steven had decided he wanted to meet me. He and a friend played hookey from school and travelled to Manhattan to find me. Through their detective work they found Melvin's studio. They rang the bell and the stylist – a young Ali McGraw, not yet the famous actress she was to become – answered the door. She was about to send them away. But Bert Stern, who was shooting a documentary on my arrival in New York for CBS at the time, overheard the conversation between Ali and the boys and thought it would make a great story for his film. He asked the two young lads to come in. I was introduced to them and apparently signed a photo for Steven, which he still has. As they left he said to his friend, 'One day I'm going to photograph Twiggy.' And in 1993 – twenty-five years later – that became a reality.

When he told me this story it brought tears to my eyes, I was so touched. It was a great beginning to our shoot together. I thank Steven for reigniting the fire and getting me back into modelling mode. Fate, I suppose. Serendipity. But how extraordinary. Another of life's circles joined up.

JOHN SWANNELL

John, another master. I could do a whole book of his work, I love it so much. He is supremely gifted and must be the ultimate gentleman photographer. He always wears a beautiful tailored suit and gorgeous brogue shoes – as opposed to the standard jeans and t-shirt usually associated with photographers. John did the photographs for my book *Twiggy: An Open Look* (*Twiggy's Guide to Looking and Feeling Great*) in 1985, and I am happy to say I have continued to work with him ever since.

The two photographs by John chosen for the book are particular favourites. Rather than do the normal, glam swimsuit shot, he had the idea of asking me to crouch in the corner like a lost waif. It's a powerful image.

I've loved all the results of our work together. John has played an important part in my career.

BRIAN ARIS

The freedom in front of a camera that I gained from working with some of those early photographers, such as Avedon, has never gone away. It created a sort of confidence in my contribution to the outcome of the collaboration.

Brian has photographed endless famous faces for various magazines, book covers and album sleeves. He was the official photographer for the Queen's seventieth birthday and her golden wedding. Most famously, he was also the official photographer for Band Aid, Live Aid and Live 8. Brian and I first worked together in 1986 and we have continued working together regularly over the years. He is the ultimate professional. I love working with him because he's fun and generates a relaxed, informal atmosphere, and I always know the results will be great. We've done so many shoots together, we have a kind of shorthand. He has a great eye for composition and his lighting is superb.

MARY McCARTNEY

Mary's mother Linda was one of my best friends. When Mary was born I made her first baby suit. She was such a sweet baby, and she has grown into a beautiful, gentle, talented woman, just like her mum. I was not at all surprised she chose to follow her mother's path as a photographer – and what a talent she has. I felt very relaxed when we worked together. Because we are friends it was easy, and I knew she knew exactly what she wanted. We were trying to create that wonderful period feel that one sees in photographs from the 1930s and '40s. Mary got the lighting spot on and once I'd put my make-up on, and got under the lights, it just fell into place and Marlene Dietrich seemed magically to appear.

ANNIE LEIBOVITZ

What a truly extraordinary person Annie is: she studied music and painting before becoming the world's most famous photographer. She achieved world recognition though her photographs for *Rolling Stone* magazine, for which she was chief photographer from 1973 to 1983, and since then has been lead photographer at *Vanity Fair*. Famously, she photographed John Lennon naked with Yoko Ono. And, more recently, Queen Elizabeth II. Annie's pictures are always immediately intriguing.

Now I'm aware that in many of my memories of working with these great photographers, I've said how nice they are – not only professionally, but also as people. Among the best is Annie Leibovitz: she's a treasure. She constantly amazes me with the way she constructs narratives and scenarios in her compositions. As usual, I was nervous about my first shoot with her, as I am with any new collaboration. Some of her work for *Rolling Stone* magazine was a bit extreme even for a child of the 1960s like me. No cause for concern though, I couldn't help loving Annie from the moment I met her, and she promised not to make me look like a gargoyle.

I worked with her first in 1998 in a sitting where she was photographing models of the twentieth century. When I arrived at her studio in New York, I was a little overwhelmed by the size of the place and the number of people involved in the shoot, but Annie quickly put me at ease and the shoot was fun and fast. We have enjoyed working together, and I hope we will continue to do so.

BRYAN ADAMS

In 2000 I got a call from Bryan Adams asking to photograph me. I'd never met him but was a huge fan of both his music and his photographs. Strange now, looking back, to think how the music world and fashion world seem to have morphed together.

The project was also something I wanted to do. Sadly, a female friend of his had died from breast cancer, and he was photographing women in the public eye for a book – in memory of his friend and to raise funds for a breast cancer charity. Having also lost my dear friend Linda McCartney to this terrible disease, I didn't hesitate to get involved.

I arrived at his studio – a fabulous converted riverside house – and we sat and had tea while we talked about the shoot. We got on like a house on fire. He's such a down to earth, friendly guy. I had brought along lots of different outfits, but in the end he chose to put a big sunhat on my head and show my bare shoulders, sitting me by a window and using natural light. We laughed a lot and he got the shot he wanted really quickly – I think the whole session only took about half an hour. He was a real pleasure to work with. And a few months later, I attended the charity auction he had organized where we raised a great deal of money, selling signed prints of the photographs.

We worked together again this year and his photographs were, as usual, brilliantly fresh and original.

MIKE OWEN

Mike started out in the music business in the latter days of the punk era, shooting bands such as Duran Duran and Spandau Ballet, and directing videos for artists including Annie Lennox.

Since his move into fashion, he has fulfilled assignments for Italian *Vogue* and *Vanity Fair*, working with Iman, Yasmin Le Bon, Kate Moss and me, as well as shooting global advertising campaigns for countless designers.

I first met Mike after he had photographed my husband Leigh in the late 1980s. Mike's style was inspired by the lighting of the great Hollywood photographers of the 1930s. The

results were truly fabulous and I so wanted
to work with him. We've since done a few shoots
together. I adore the picture we've included with
the lace across my face. We shot it at the Savoy
Hotel in London and I was wearing a fabulous
Ronit Zilkha outfit. Mike is another master of
lighting and composition, and not only in colour;
in my opinion his black-and-white portraits rank
among the best.

SØLVE SUNDSBØ

Imagine my surprise and delight at the grand
old age of fifty-nine to be asked to be on the
cover of *i-D* magazine, a brilliant, young, hip and
innovative publication. It was a special issue put
together by the inspiring fashion director Edward
Enninful, celebrating the Best of British in
fashion. The shoot was a mammoth undertaking,
requiring sessions in London and New York.

When I arrived at the studio in north London
I was amazed at how many people were involved.
Sølve ran the sessions like clockwork. I was a
little nervous at first, as I always am when
working with a new photographer, but once
I got in front of the camera, I relaxed – I knew
by the lighting that he was going to get great
pictures. My session overlapped with Kate Moss's.
After hugging and kissing and having a glass of
champagne with Kate, Sølve asked if we'd do
a shoot together, and it's one of my favourites.
Kate is adorable and the best. Sølve captured
a wonderful moment in time.

1966 | Ronald Traeger

PORTRAITS

1967 | **Barry Lategan**

1974 | Barry Lategan

1967 | Bert Stern

1967 | **Bert Stern**

1967 | Melvin Sokolsky

1967 | Melvin Sokolsky

1967 | Melvin Sokolsky

1967 | **Richard Avedon**

1967 | **Richard Avedon**

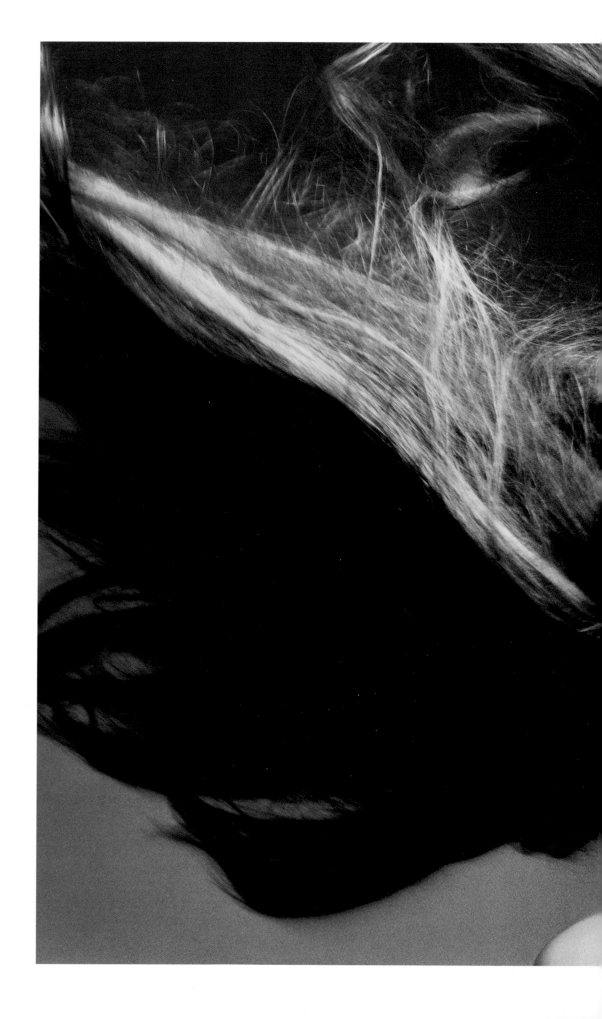

1968 | Richard Avedon

1967 | **Richard Avedon**

1983 | Francesco Scavullo

1967 | Francesco Scavullo

1967 | Ronald Traeger

1967 | Ronald Traeger

1967 | Cecil Beaton

70

1968 | Cecil Beaton

1973 | Justin de Villeneuve

1968 | Justin de Villeneuve

1969 | **Linda McCartney**

1970 | **Douglas Kirkland**

1971 | Douglas Kirkland

mid 1970s | **Norman Parkinson**

1975 | Terry O'Neill

1983 | Steven Meisel

1993 | Steven Meisel

1996 | Brian Aris

1986 | Brian Aris

2000 | Mary McCartney

CHRONOLOGY

1949

On 19 September Twiggy is born Lesley Hornby, in north-west London, third daughter of Helen (Nellie) Lydia Hornby (née Reeman) and William Norman Hornby and sister to Shirley and Vivien (*fig. 1*).

1950

As a baby, aged about ten months, Twiggy comes third in Willesden Carnival beautiful baby contest (*fig. 2*).

1957

Her first appearance in the press aged seven: Twiggy is one of twenty-four pupils invited to a Park Lane hotel for doing something of which they were proud. 'Pretty Miss Lesley Hornby of Willesden' had entered a painting in the children's art competition for the *Sunday Pictorial* newspaper.

1960

Twiggy attends Bridge Road Junior School, London NW10, where she learns to read music and play the recorder (*fig. 3*). She is taught dressmaking by her mother.

1961

Twiggy starts at Brondesbury and Kilburn High School for Girls in Salusbury Road, Kilburn (*fig. 4*).

1963-4

Twiggy becomes a Mod and goes to dances with a gang of girlfriends wearing fitted suits with mid-calf. tight skirts, nylon macs and Hush Puppies. Her design and sewing skills help her to keep up with the ever-changing Mod fashions.

She goes to see The Beatles play at Finsbury Park Astoria, London.

1964-5

At her Saturday job at local hairdresser Mr Vincent's, a fellow hairdresser nicknames the young Lesley Hornby 'Sticks', which then becomes 'Twiggy', because of her skinny legs. She uses her money to shop at Biba; her Mod fashion icon is Cathy McGowan, host of *Ready Steady Go*.

1

2

3

4

1966

The first credited photograph of Twiggy (by Lewis Morley) appears in print in the *London Life* in January (*fig. 5*): 'Lesley (Twiggy) Hornby in the Chelsea Antique Market in the coat she bought in the Portobello Road for £5.'

'I feel very ashamed at wearing fur, but I can only plead the ignorance of youth. I have not worn fur personally or professionally for over thirty-five years and campaign strongly against it.'

In February Susan Robbins at *Women's Mirror* offers Twiggy a year's contract for beauty and head shots at £9 a week. Noted hairdresser Leonard cuts Twiggy's hair into the famous boyish crop. Barry Lategan photographs her with her new hairstyle (*fig. 6*). The shots are displayed in Leonard's salon, where they are seen by Deirdre McSharry of the *Daily Express*.

6

5

Fashion report by Theo Goldrey

WHAT PEOPLE ARE WEARING

Susannah York in a black crepe trouser suit from Top Gear by Foale & Tuffin, and an ostrich feather boa from John Lewis   Lesley (Twiggy) Hornby in the Chelsea Antique Market in the raccoon coat she bought in Portobello Road for £5

7

Fashion editor Deirdre McSharry profiles Twiggy and interviews her for the *Daily Express*. 'Twiggy: The Cockney Kid with the face to launch a thousand shapes ... And she's only 16!' is published on 3 February. McSharry declares: 'THIS IS THE FACE OF '66 ... just 16, Cockney-pert and with the stamp of "now". THIS IS THE NAME, Twiggy (yes, really) because she is branch slim, bends to every shape in fashion and has her hair cut like a cap made of leaves. THIS IS THE LOOK that from this moment will launch thousands of clothes, a craze for freckles, dozens of hairpieces, and will cause a sellout in eye pencils.' The article is illustrated with two photographs by Barry Lategan, one with her short crop and a second with a long, false plait of fair hair (*fig. 7*). 'It was meant to be the new, hot thing,' says Twiggy. Another photograph, by *Express* staff photographer Norman Potter, shows Twiggy full length in an ensemble she had designed herself.

Twiggy asks her parents permission to leave school and model full-time. Articles by Robin Douglas-Hume and William Hickey appear on subsequent days, criticizing Twiggy's figure and the 'hero-worship' of models and photographers.

Twiggy's modelling career takes off. She appears in print in numerous magazines, including *Honey*, *Petticoat*, *Fabulous*, *Look*, *Brides* and *Woman*.

One of Twiggy's earliest published fashion stories over several pages appears in *Petticoat* on 9 April, photographed by Barry Lategan, with hair by House of Leonard.

Pictures of Twiggy, taken 16–17 February by David Montgomery, are published in April's edition of British *Vogue*.

'Twiggy Talking … as she rockets (all 6½ stone of her) to the top in modelling' – Peter Senn's interview is published in the *Daily Mirror*: 'I can't believe it when I see pictures of myself. It has all

happened so quickly. The photographers are very nice. They always get me dancing or jumping. And I think the other models are smashing.'

Guy Bourdin's photographs of Twiggy, taken on 11 March, are published in French *Vogue* in May. She appears in September's *Elle* magazine (fig. 8).

The Times reports that Twiggy is invited to the Women of the Year lunch, and in October she appears on the cover of *Honey* (fig. 9).

Twiggy launches Twiggy Dresses, which she models at the press view. Deirdre McSharry writes in the *Daily Express* that a factory covering eight acres has been bought to manufacture Twiggy's clothing line ('The Dizzy Success Story of Twiggy: 8 acres to push her look').

In December Twiggy is included in the *Daily Mirror*'s 'End of year report on a place called Swinging Britain', and *Petticoat* announces 'To Twiggy – Model of 1966 Award'.

The eponymous *Twiggy* magazines appear (figs 10, 11). 'How does Twiggy herself feel about the fashion revolution she has caused? "It's like reading about somebody else," she says.'

Adel Rootstein designs a Twiggy mannequin, which appears in shop windows everywhere. *Twiggy* magazine pictures her with the mannequin, wearing her clothing designs (fig. 12).

She is photographed taking children to the circus (fig. 13). 'Britain's top model,

8

9

10

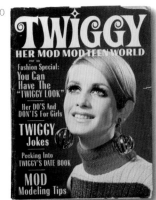

11

12

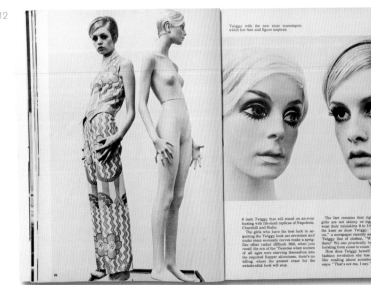

Twiggy, aged 17, played "mum" to 50 children at Bertram Mills Circus, Olympia, today. The children who came from Lambeth mission were entertained by Bertram Mills and the Save the Children Fund.'

Madame Tussauds adds a model of Twiggy to its hall of fame. Ronald Traeger pictures her at Tussauds with a model of Muhammad Ali (fig. 14). The Twiggy Doll is launched by Mattel, makers of Barbie (fig. 15).

Twiggy is sent to Paris in January to cover the summer collections for the *Daily Sketch*. 'I had imagined a vast room with a catwalk and toffee-nosed models eight feet high and granite-faced women gliding about in grand clothes. Not a bit of that. Louis Feraud's salon is so tiny that people were standing and sitting on the stairs. There was hardly any room left for the models, who were all very young and friendly, to squeeze between us. The clothes were super … Beautifully cut, very

narrow on the shoulders, slim but not flat-chested, with lots of double rows of stitching emphasizing the seams ….'

Suzy Menkes outlines in *The Times* 'Fashion Extra' the idea of labelling a product with the name of a well-known personality. Twiggy's clothing line is mentioned and Menkes describes her involvement in the process: 'Twiggy says whether she likes them or not; whether she feels her generation will wear them.'

In February *Life* magazine includes 'The Arrival of Twiggy' by Jean Claude Sauer. The *Daily Mirror*'s front page has an article by Jean Dobson. 'Tycoon Twiggy'.

Twiggy makes her first trip to America in March, where the height of Twiggymania is documented by photographer and film-maker Bert Stern for ABC Television: 'Twiggy in New York', 'Twiggy in Hollywood', 'Twiggy, Why?'. She is mobbed on Fifth Avenue and followed by crowds of fans. Twiggy is welcomed to LA by a party thrown for her by Sonny and Cher. Stern photographs her for US *Vogue* and she appears on the cover.

15

13

14

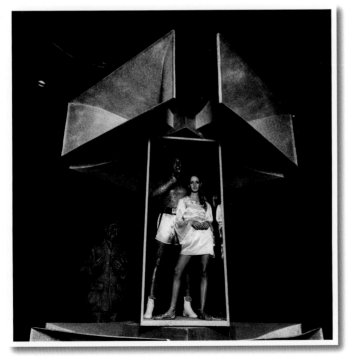

A major profile of Twiggy appears in *Newsweek* (USA), published on 10 April, with a portrait by Bert Stern on the cover (*fig. 16*).

Twiggy flies hairdresser Leonard to New York (*fig. 17*). 'Twiggy with hair remodelled. New York: British model Twiggy (real name Lesley Hornby) seen April 12 when she had her hair modelled by London hair-stylist Leonard after she flew him in at a cost of £254:11s. Cost of the hairdo was three guineas. Twiggy is currently modelling British fashions in the United States.'

She models for *Elle* magazine, photographed by Marc Hispard (*fig. 18*).

17

16

18

Twiggy appears on the cover of the May edition of French *Vogue*, photographed by Henry Clarke.

Photographs by Melvin Sokolsky are selected for the cover of *Ladies' Home Journal* in June (*fig. 19*). The inside pages include the Rainbow dress as worn in Norman Parkinson's BBC documentary 'Stay Baby Stay', part of the *One Pair of Eyes* series, in which Twiggy is seen dancing to 'Jimmy Mack' by Martha and the Vandellas (currently one of the most watched Twiggy items on YouTube).

Seventeen puts Twiggy on the cover in July (photographed by Carmen Schiavone, *fig. 20*). She is photographed for the cover of *McCalls* by Otto Storch. She is again on the cover of *Seventeen* in September (Joseph Santoro).

In both July and August she graces the cover of US *Vogue*, photographed by Richard Avedon in March that year. For the July edition she has flowers painted around her eyes; she wears a green and white top for August (*fig. 21*).

In August *Petticoat* runs an article on Twiggy and Jean Shrimpton, describing Twiggy as 'comparable to the Beatles: as the Beatles had a profound effect on the way the Englishman looked, so Twiggy's appearance affected the appearance of the English girl. Tailor's dummies in shop windows now look like Twiggy: the girls in the street look like Twiggy. Twiggy is not extraordinary – she is a child of her time. She and her contemporaries had what had formerly been denied to the working class girl – an utter certainty of how they should look, and how they should behave. That is what poise means ...'.

In October Twiggy flies to Japan to show Twiggy collections over a three-week tour. While she is away in Japan she is featured on the cover of the *Daily Telegraph Magazine* (3 November), photographed by Bill King. Photographs by Barry Lategan of her 1930s looks and by John Adriaan of her 1920s looks are published in the *Daily Mirror* ('Terribly Modern Twiggy').

Twiggy's own look takes on a more 1930s feel, which is shown on the cover of December's *Look* magazine (*fig. 22*). 'I stopped wearing short skirts more or less completely around October 1967.'

19

20

21

22

1968

Twiggy by Twiggy, a pictorial autobiography, is published by Hawthorn Books (USA), announcing her as 'an international phenomenon and the symbol *par excellence* of the 1960s' (*fig. 23*). Diana Vreeland, editor-in-chief of *Vogue*, is quoted: 'Twiggy is completely disarming and charming ... She is the mini-girl in the mini-camera. She's delicious-looking.' It is translated into German as *Twiggy Über Twiggy* the following year.

Richard Avedon photographs Twiggy at the Paris collections in January. These pictures, also featuring Penelope Tree, appear in US *Vogue*'s 'Eye View' – 'Two Girls in Paris: the Twig and the Tree'.

Twiggy travels Europe to promote her clothing line, visiting Germany in March and Sweden in May (*fig. 24*). 'TWIGGY PLAYS BOTH BONNIE AND CLYDE: Twiggy wears a jersey cardigan and culottes with matching beret – from the Twiggy summer collection shown in London today.'

Photographs by André Berg appear in July's *Mademoiselle Age Tendre* of Twiggy wearing a kimono (*figs 25, 26*).

Cecil Beaton's portrait of Twiggy is included in 'Beaton Portraits 1928–1968', the first photographic exhibition ever staged at the National Portrait Gallery, London, which opens in October to record attendance figures.

Queen magazine's May edition features the 'Five Faces of Twiggy', dressed as Rita Hayworth, Greta Garbo, Theda Bara, Marilyn Monroe and Ginger Rogers. The wigs are by Leonard; photographs by Justin de Villenueve, who uses tungsten lighting to give the pictures a 1930s feel. The images are picked up and syndicated worldwide (*figs 27, 28, 29*).

Twiggy launches Twiggy Tights (*fig. 30*). 'Being shown in London this morning was a new range of tights being launched by fashion model Twiggy. All the designs have been personally approved by Twiggy, and several of them are of her own design.'

Richard Avedon's colourized versions of the Four Seasons shots appear in *McCalls* magazine in March.

In April *The Times* pictures a Twiggy mural on the new *QEII*, designed by two former Royal College of Art students.

For the first time, Twiggy is captured on film singing and dancing, in a lavishly produced advertisement for Diet Rite cola, filmed at Wembley by Melvin Sokolsky (*fig. 31*). The *Daily Mirror* publishes: 'At Last, The Singin' Dancin' Actin' Twiggy Show'.

Thames Television airs Twiggy's *This Is Your Life* in December. She is the youngest person to appear on the biographical chat programme.

Ken Russell, whom she had met two years earlier, casts Twiggy as Polly Browne in the musical film *The Boy Friend*. This is the beginning of her change of career.

'It was like walking into *The Secret Garden*. I loved the whole process. A whole new world had opened up for me.'

Douglas Kirkland photographs 'The Now Blooming Twiggy' for *Look* magazine in May.

On holiday in Jamaica Twiggy meets Noël Coward, whose writing will inform her stage repertoire (*fig. 32*).

'I thought I'd lost this photo. About twenty-five years later I rediscovered it when I was cleaning a bookshelf and it fell out from the pages of a book. A month after that I was offered the role of Elvira in Noël Coward's *Blithe Spirit* at Chichester Festival Theatre. Amazing.'

31

30

32

1971

Ken Russell's film version of Sandy Wilson's musical *The Boy Friend*, in which Twiggy takes her first lead role, is released by Metro-Goldwyn-Mayer. Russell's wife Shirley designs the costumes, and Tony Walton designs the sets, which are photographed by Douglas Kirkland. Twiggy takes nine months of dance lessons to prepare for the role (*figs 33, 34, 35*).

The Times describes *The Boy Friend* as 'Twiggy's metamorphosis from a giggling, gawky girl of 1966 into a capable, talented actress.'

33

35

34

1971

'Twiggy CAN act' proclaims *The Australian Women's Weekly* on its July front cover, with a picture of her in *The Boy Friend* (fig. 36).

The US premiere of *The Boy Friend* goes well, and the London *Times* reports 'New York critics friendly to Twiggy film' (figs 37, 38).

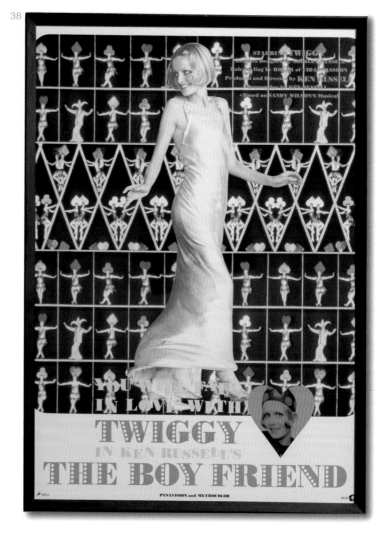

1972

The royal premiere of *The Boy Friend* takes place at the Empire Cinema, Leicester Square, London in January. The *Sunday Times Magazine* puts Twiggy, dressed in her role as Polly Browne, on its front cover, and reproduces Douglas Kirkland's film stills inside, with additional images by Nigel Coates (*fig. 39*).

1973

Twiggy wins two Golden Globes for her role in *The Boy Friend*: Most Promising Newcomer – Female, and Best Motion Picture Actress – Musical/Comedy (*fig. 40*). She appears on the cover of *Film Review* in March.

Returning to British *Vogue* for an interview with Polly Devlin, published in September, Twiggy begins to assert control over her new career. She is shot for the cover by Barry Lategan (*fig. 41*).

Twiggy is on the cover of British *Vogue* again in April (*fig. 42*).

39

40

41

42

1973

Twiggy and David Bowie are shot together for British *Vogue*, but, reluctant to feature a man on the cover, *Vogue* dismisses the photographs.

'I told them that David Bowie was possibly the only man in the world you could credit the make-up on.'

Bowie uses the image on the cover of his album *Pin Ups* released in October (*fig. 43*). Bowie had referenced 'Twig the Wonder Kid' in the lyrics of his 1972 song 'Drive-In Saturday' from the album *Aladdin Sane*.

1974

Twiggy stars with Michael Whitney in the film thriller *W*, directed by Richard Quinne and produced by Audrey Hepburn's husband Mel Ferrer (*fig. 44*).

Television series *Twiggs* (BBC) is a success and a further series is scheduled for the following summer.

Twiggy makes her stage debut in the lead role as Cinderella at the Casino Theatre, London, in December. The *Daily Mail* reports that 'there is a magic aura of originality about her that can only be summed up as star-plus.' The costumes are designed by Barbara Hulanicki of Biba. Barry Lategan's photograph of Twiggy in the role is the cover of British *Vogue*.

43

44

1975

The cover of *Plays and Players* shows 'Twiggy's Cinderella', shot by Justin de Villeneuve (*fig. 45*).

Hart-Davis, MacGibbon (London) publishes a new autobiography, *Twiggy*, with cover photographs by Justin de Villeneuve (front) and Barry Lategan (back) (*fig. 46*).

Twiggy spends time in the USA, making appearances on television and at parties in New York (*fig. 48*).

'I was appearing on a very popular American chat show and the other guests were the Jackson Five. At the time my niece Tracy was a huge fan. I knew I'd be her favourite auntie if I went back with a picture and I got her a signed one. Apart from his extraordinary talent, Michael was a really charming, sweet boy.' (*fig. 47*).

48

45
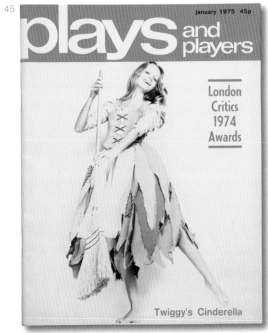

47

46
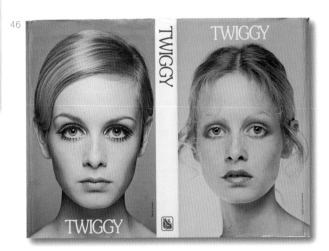

1976

Twiggy is signed to Mercury records and releases the album *Twiggy*, produced by Tony Eyers, gaining a silver disc for sales (*figs 49, 50*). The album includes her top-twenty hit single 'Here I Go Again'. Twiggy sings on *Top of the Pops*, *Supersonic* and *The Muppet Show*, and tours Britain with the album, culminating in a sell-out show at the Royal Albert Hall, London. She is featured on the cover of *Record Mirror*.

1977

Twiggy tours the UK promoting her new album, *Please Get My Name Right* (Mercury, *fig. 51*). *Meet* magazine features a giveaway giant poster of Twiggy.

Twiggy marries Michael Whitney on 14 June. The marriage lasts until his early death in 1983. Daughter Carly is born on 1 December at Queen Charlotte's Maternity Hospital, Hammersmith.

Twiggy appears on *Bing Crosby's Merrie Olde Christmas* (*fig. 52*), his last Christmas special, dueting with him on 'Have Yourself a Merry Little Christmas' (later released, in 1982). David Bowie is a guest on the same programme, singing 'Little Drummer Boy'.

49

50

52

51

1980

Hit film *The Blues Brothers*, directed by John Landis, features a cameo from Twiggy playing a 'chic lady' who catches the eye of Elwood Blues, played by Dan Ackroyd (*fig. 53*).

Twiggy tells Michael Parkinson on his chat show about recording studio sessions with Donna Summer and Juergen Koppers.

1981

ITV screens *Pygmalion*, a Yorkshire Television production in which Twiggy plays Eliza Doolittle opposite Robert Powell's Henry Higgins (*figs 54, 55*).

'I just did me and leant on the Cockney – not that I was a real Cockney. But then neither was Eliza. She was from north-west London, like me.'

1983

Twiggy appears on the front cover of Andy Warhol's *Interview* magazine, photographed by Cris Alexander, designed and painted by Richard Bernstein (*fig. 56*). 'Twiggy, Co-starring with Tommy Tune in *My One and Only*', Opening in Boston and Headed for Broadway this March.'

55

53

56

54

1983-4

On 1 May 1983 the musical *My One and Only* opens on Broadway at St James's Theater on West 44th Street (*figs 57, 58*). After months of rehearsals and under the direction of Mike Nichols, the show, a story based around Gershwin's back catalogue, is a success. During final rehearsals in April *The Times* asks, 'It's like Fred and Ginger all over again ... innit?' Ginger Rogers later comes to see the show (*fig. 59*).

At the opening night party Twiggy and her co-star Tommy Tune meet Laurence Olivier and his wife Joan Plowright (*fig. 60*). The following morning she receives a note on headed paper from the Carlyle Hotel:

'My Lovely Twiglet
What a sweet joy it was to meet last night, having adored you from afar. I am so deep in admiration for your talent, which seems to gain strides every year – every hour. Joan and I do congratulate you from our very warmest hearts and wish you more and more success at the same rate.
Ever and ever
Your
Larry'

My One and Only wins three Tony Awards, and Twiggy is nominated for Best Actress in a Musical.

61

57

60

58

Noted members of the audience include Gene Kelly and Julie Andrews (*fig. 61*).

'At one point the script had us marooned on a desert island. It had been Tommy's dream to tap dance in water – a bit like Gene Kelly in *Singing in the Rain* – and this was the perfect opportunity. We were barefoot and did tap steps, but instead of 'tap tap', they went 'slosh slosh', water going everywhere. It was more for effect than the sound and it always brought the house down' (*fig. 62*).

Twiggy and Carly are photographed in New York (*fig. 63*).

62

59

63

1984

Twiggy appears on *Bob Hope's Super Birthday Special* on NBC (*fig. 64*).

Twiggy meets Carly Simon, after whom she had named her daughter, and records a duet later released on her 2003 album *Midnight Blue* (*fig. 65*).

1985

Twiggy appears in Twentieth Century Fox's *The Doctor and the Devils*. Based on a novel by Dylan Thomas, it is directed by Freddie Francis and stars Timothy Dalton, Jonathan Pryce and Stephen Rae (*fig. 66*).

Feel Emotion is released by Arista. The cover image shows Twiggy while filming *Club Paradise* in Jamaica (*fig. 67*).

1986

Club Paradise, directed by Harold Ramis, sees Twiggy in a Warner Brothers film comedy alongside Robin Williams, Peter O'Toole and Rick Moranis (*fig. 68*).

68

64

66

Copyright © 1985 20th Century-Fox Film Corporation. All rights reserved. Permission is hereby granted to newspapers and other periodicals to reproduce this photograph for publicity or advertising except for the endorsement of products. This must not be sold, leased or given away. Printed in U.S.A.

Graverobbers Fallon (**JONATHAN PRYCE**, top right) and Broom (**STEPHEN RAE**, top left) menace Jenny, a young prostitute played by **TWIGGY**, in Twentieth Century Fox's "**THE DOCTOR AND THE DEVILS**," a gothic thriller from the pen of Dylan Thomas.

65

67
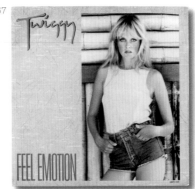

1988

Twiggy stars in *Madame Sousatska*, directed by John Schlesinger. The all-star cast includes Shirley MacLaine, Peggy Ashcroft, Shabana Amzi and Leigh Lawson (*figs 69, 70*).

Later that year, on 23 September, Twiggy marries Leigh Lawson in the garden of Tony Walton's house at Sag Harbor, Long Island (*fig. 71*).

1989

Television series *The Young Charlie Chaplin*, directed by Baz Taylor, sees Twiggy playing Chaplin's mother, alongside Ian McShane.

1990

Mats Arehn directs Twiggy in *Istanbul (Keep Your Eyes Open)*.

71

69

70

1993

Twiggy appears on the cover of the April edition of Italian *Vogue* entitled 'Il Mito' – The Legend (*fig. 72*). In her first fashion editorial for nearly twenty-five years, she is photographed by Steven Meisel. The pictures run over several interior pages.

Meisel's shoot encourages Twiggy back into modelling and she is placed on the cover of *Tatler* in September. The cover flags a major pictorial feature on Twiggy as photographed by Barry Lategan. The story includes old contact sheets and new shots of Twiggy with daughter Carly and husband Leigh.

72

VOGUE

ITALIA

A P R.
1993
N. 512
L. 7.500

IL MITO

Twiggy

CAMICIA ALBERTA FERRETTI

1995

Twiggy attends the opening of Richard Avedon's show *Evidence 1944–1994* at the National Portrait Gallery, London, on 21 March. She is pictured with the photographer in front of a large version of autumn from his 1968 Four Seasons shoot (*fig. 73*).

1996

Twiggy releases the album *London Pride* (Varese Sarabande).

'Linda, me, Kate Moss and Stella McCartney. A favourite photo captured at a private party hosted by dear friends Paul and Linda McCartney.' (*fig. 74*)

1997

An updated autobiography, with Penelope Dening, is published by Simon & Schuster, *Twiggy: In Black and White* (*fig. 75*). Cover photographs are by Brian Aris, who also shoots Leigh, Carly, Twiggy and stepson Jason for *Hello* magazine (*fig. 76*).

Treading the boards at Chichester Festival Theatre, Twiggy plays Elvira in Noël Coward's *Blithe Spirit*. She is well reviewed in *The Stage*: 'Twiggy Lawson, as the deliciously haunting Elvira, excels in her responses to the situation.'

1998

Twiggy hosts her own television show, *Twiggy's People* (Granada).

At Bay Street Theatre, Long Island, New York, she stars in the musical *Noël and Gertie*, which prefigures *If Love Were All*, adapted and directed by Leigh Lawson the following year.

The Best of Twiggy is released, featuring the entire *Twiggy* album (1976) and highlights from *Please Get My Name Right* (1977).

1999

From June to September Twiggy stars as Gertrude Lawrence, appearing opposite Harry Groener as Noël Coward in the play *If Love Were All* at the Lucille Lortel Theater, New York (*fig. 77*).

Annie Leibovitz photographs 'The Übermodels' for November's US *Vogue*. Twiggy appears alongside Lauren Hutton, Penelope Tree, Veruschka and the hottest models of the day.

73

77

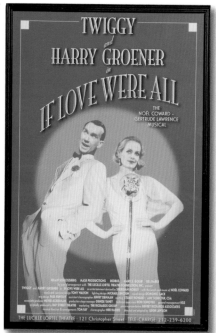

75

76

74

2000

The Times Magazine puts Twiggy on the cover with Kate Moss, photographed by Brigitte Lacombe, for its millennium edition, published 1 January (*fig. 78*).

Twiggy is photographed by John Swannell in front of the iconic Barry Lategan photograph that launched her career (*fig. 79*).

2001

Twiggy hosts *Take Time with Twiggy* (ITV). She makes a guest appearance on comedy show *Absolutely Fabulous*, starring Joanna Lumley and Jennifer Saunders (*fig. 80*).

November's *Professional Photographer* magazine runs 'They Shot Twiggy – Photographers who made and kept her famous', with a Mike Owen cover.

2002

Reprising the role for a summer run, Twiggy stars as Elvira in Noël Coward's *Blithe Spirit* at Bay Street Theatre, Long Island, New York. 'Twiggy is a magnificent hallucination, a classic Elvira of the spirits.' says *The New York Times*.

2003

Twiggy releases *Midnight Blue*, featuring previously unreleased material, including duets with Carly Simon and Leo Sayer, recorded from 1982 to 1990.

Twiggy stars in Sir Peter Hall's production of *Mrs Warren's Profession*, touring the UK throughout May, June and July (*fig. 81*).

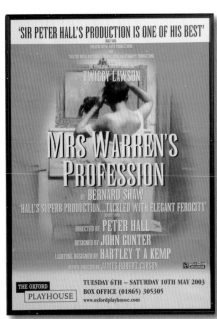

2005

Twiggy fronts a major new television, press and billboard campaign for British department store Marks & Spencer, with Noemie Lenoir, Laura Bailey and Erin O'Connor (*fig. 82*).

Twiggy joins the cast of Tyra Banks's television show *America's Next Top Model* (UPN/The CW) as one of four judges. Twiggy stays with the series for 62 episodes (*fig. 83*).

2006

BBC Radio 4's *Afternoon Play* series features 'Elevenses with Twiggy', written by Simon Farquhar, in which she plays herself as a nineteen-year-old girl.

In November, *Harper's Bazaar* runs a feature on Twiggy, 'A Life in Style'.

Vogue celebrates its ninetieth birthday. A photograph of Twiggy from the M&S campaign is published in the birthday issue, on which she writes 'Happy Birthday! – Still in Vogue' (*fig. 84*).

2007

Twiggy is signed to London agency Models 1.

84

83

82

2008

Twiggy: A Guide to Looking and Feeling Fabulous Over Forty is published by Penguin (*fig. 85*) with cover photographs by Brian Aris, who also shoots mother and daughter together (*fig. 86*). Carly celebrates her thirtieth birthday (pictured here with guests Paul McCartney and Nancy Shevell, *fig. 87*).

Television programme *Twiggy's Frock Exchange* airs on BBC 2 in October.

Twiggy supports the 'Fashion Targets Breast Cancer' campaign in support of Breakthrough Breast Cancer. Posters show her in the campaign t-shirt, photographed by Rankin.

2009

In March the style magazine *i-D* puts Twiggy on the cover, photographed by Sølve Sundsbø (*fig. 88*).

Twiggy is guest of honour and poster girl at the prestigious Metropolitan Museum of Art's annual Costume Institute Benefit in New York. The gala event marks the opening of a new exhibition celebrating 'The Model as Muse', running from 6 May to 9 August. Twiggy is an honorary member of the exhibitions committee, chaired by Marc Jacobs, with co-chairs Kate Moss, Justin Timberlake and Anna Wintour, editor-in-chief of US *Vogue*.

In July Twiggy is announced as the new face of Olay Definity, twenty-five years after she first became the face of Oil of Ulay (*fig. 89*).

To coincide with her sixtieth birthday on 19 September, *Twiggy: A Life in Photographs* opens in Room 33 at the National Portrait Gallery, London.

89

86

88

85
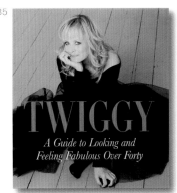

87

FILM, STAGE, MUSIC AND BOOKS

FILM AND TELEVISION

The Boy Friend (GB 1971)

'W' (USA, 1974)

There Goes the Bride (GB, 1979)

The Blues Brothers (US, 1980)

Pygmalion (GB television, 1981)

The Doctor and the Devils (GB, 1985)

Club Paradise (US, 1986)

The Little Match Girl (GB television, 1986)

Madame Sousatzka (GB, 1988)

The Diamond Trap (US television, 1988)

Sun Child (GB television, 1988)

Young Charlie Chaplin (GB television, 1989)

Istanbul (aka *Keep Your Eyes Open*)
(Sweden, 1990)

Body Bags (US television, 1993)

Something Borrowed, Something Blue
(US television, 1998)

Woundings (GB/US, 1998)

Absolutely Fabulous (GB television series, 2001)

The Taming of the Shrew – Shakespeare Re-Told
(GB television, 2005)

STAGE

Cinderella (pantomime)
Casino Theatre, London, December 1974

The Butterfly Ball
The Royal Albert Hall, London, 16 October 1975

Captain Beaky and His Musical Christmas
(pantomime)
Apollo Victoria Theatre, London, December 1981

My One and Only
St. James Theater, New York, 1 May 1983 to
31 October 1984

Blithe Spirit
Chichester Festival Theatre, 11 June to 3 August
1997; Bay Street Theatre, Long Island, New York,

16 July to 4 August 2002

Noël and Gertie
Bay Street Theatre, Long Island, New York, 1998

If Love Were All
Lucille Lortel Theater, New York, 10 June to
5 September 1999

The Play What I Wrote
Wyndham's Theatre, London, 19–25 March and
6–7 December 2002; Theatre Royal, Newcastle,
15–16 October 2002

Mrs Warren's Profession
English tour, May–July 2003

MUSIC

Albums, unless otherwise indicated.

The Boy Friend – Promotional Radio Interview
(1971)

The Boy Friend – Original Soundtrack Recording
(1971)

'A Room in Bloomsbury' (with Christopher Gable)
/ 'You Are My Lucky Star' / 'All I Do Is Dream of
You' (7-inch single, 1971)

Cole Porter in Paris (1973)

Twiggy (1976)

Captain Beaky and His Band (1977)

My One and Only – Original Broadway Cast
Recording (1983)

The Doctor and the Devils – Original Soundtrack
(7-inch, with Twiggy singing 'Whisper and I Shall
Hear', 1985)

More Whodunnits (audio book, 1995)

London Pride – Songs from the London Stage
(1996)

Dead Man on Campus – Original Soundtrack
(1998)

The Best of Twiggy (1998)

If Love Were All – Original Cast Recording (1999)

Midnight Blue (2003)

Gotta Sing, Gotta Dance (2009)

BOOKS

*Twiggy: A Guide to Looking Good and Feeling
Fabulous over Forty* (Penguin, 2008)

Twiggy in Black and White by Twiggy Lawson
and Penelope Denning (Simon & Schuster, 1997)

Twiggy's Guide to Looking Good by Twiggy
and Angela Neustatter (Robson Books, 1985)

Twiggy autobiography (Hart-Davis/MacGibbon
Ltd, 1975)

Twiggy by Twiggy (Hawthorn Books Inc., 1968)

Further details can be found at
www.twiggylawson.co.uk

NOTES

'SUPER NEW THING' BY ROBIN MUIR

1. Polly Devlin, 'Paris: Twiggy Haute Couture', American *Vogue*, 15 March 1967, p.65.
2. 'Twiggy – Prête à Porter', American *Vogue*, 15 February 1967, p.100.
3. Cecil Beaton, quoted in 'Twiggy: Click! Click!', *Newsweek*, 10 April 1967, p.65.
4. Justin de Villeneuve, quoted in Thomas Whiteside, 'A Reporter at Large. A Super New Thing', *The New Yorker*, 4 November 1967, p.66
5. Ibid., p.64.
6. Ibid., p.74.
7. 'The Arrival of Twiggy', *Life*, 27 January 1967, p.48 et seq., and 'Fashion Model Twiggy Close-up', *Life*, 3 February 1967, p.40.
8. *Newsweek*, op. cit., p.62.
9. 'Ils Recrêent la Femme', French *Vogue*, May 1966 (taken 11 March 1966).
10. 'Young Idea. Great Little Evenings', British *Vogue*, 1 October 1966 (taken 15 August 1966).
11. 'Young Idea. World View. The Great Young Internationals', British *Vogue*, 15 April 1966 (taken 16–17 February 1966).
12. British *Vogue*, 1 March 1967 (taken 10 January 1967).
13. Helmut Newton for British *Vogue*: 'Young Idea. Lights Up Dark', 15 March 1967 (taken 16 January 1967); 'Young Idea. Six O'Clock Change', 1 April 1967. Just Jaeckin for British *Vogue*: 'Legs', 15 April 1967 and 'The Sun and You', May 1967 (both taken 10 February 1967). For Jaeckin's unpublished session, see Robin Derrick and Robin Muir, *Unseen Vogue: The Secret History of Fashion Photography* (Little, Brown, London, 2002) pp.146–7.
14. 'Un Été en Robes de Guipure', French *Vogue*, May 1967.
15. 'Paris: Twiggy Haute Couture', American *Vogue*, 15 March 1967, and 'Twiggy: Le Mannequin-Vedette 1967', French *Vogue*, April 1967.
16. Ronald Traeger for British *Vogue*: 'Young Idea's Darling Buds of May', May 1967 (taken 8–9 February 1967). Sieff for British *Vogue*: 'Young Idea's Green Belt Girl', 15 October 1967 (taken spring 1967).
17. Richardson's 'Accessories' session was early 1967.
18. Quoted in Whiteside, op. cit., p.65.
19. Ibid., p.101.
20. American *Vogue*, 1 August 1967, p.49.
21. Barbara Thorbahn, quoted in Whiteside, op. cit., p.90.
22 Devlin, op. cit., p.147.
23. Robin Douglas-Home, *Daily Express*, 24 February 1966, p.8.
24. Marshall McLuhan, quoted in *Newsweek*, op. cit., p.65.
25. Charlotte Curtis, quoted in Whiteside, op. cit., p.77.
26. 'Paris: Twiggy Haute Couture', op. cit., p.65 (caption).
27. *Twiggy by Twiggy* (Hawthorn Books, New York, 1968) p.88. Sokolsky's photographs became part of an insert booklet for synthetic fibres manufactured by The Monsanto Company and published in *Women's Wear Daily*.
28. *Newsweek*, op. cit., p.62.
29. See *Twiggy by Twiggy*, op. cit., p.69; *Twiggy: An Autobiography* (Hart-Davis, MacGibbon, London, 1975), p.53; *Twiggy in Black and White: An Autobiography* (Simon & Schuster, London, 1997), p.74.
30. Richard Avedon quoted in Whiteside, op. cit., p.150.
31. Twiggy quoted in Whiteside, op. cit., p.149; *Twiggy in Black and White: An Autobiography*, op. cit., p.80.
32. Avedon quoted in Whiteside, op. cit., p.149 (both quotes).
33. Newton for British *Vogue*: 'Young Idea's Dandy Look', September 1967 (taken 6 June 1967); Beaton for British *Vogue*: 'Young Idea's Flight of Fancy Dress', 1 October 1967 (taken 5 July 1967).
34. Beaton from his diaries, quoted in Hugo Vickers, *Cecil Beaton: The Authorised Biography* (Weidenfeld & Nicolson, London, 1985) p.514.
35. Cecil Beaton, 'Spotlight: The Changing Face of the Model', British *Vogue*, 15 March 1967, p.108.
36. Diana Vreeland, quoted in *Newsweek*, op. cit., p.65.
37. Vreeland, quoted in Michael Gross, *Model: The Ugly Business of Beautiful Women* (William Morrow & Company, 1995), p.182.
38. Vreeland memorandum, quoted in Whiteside, op. cit., pp.150–1.
39. Peter Evans in *Goodbye Baby and Amen: A Saraband for the Sixties* (Condé Nast Books, 1969), p.172; *Newsweek*, op. cit., p.62.
40. Twiggy, quoted in Leslie Bennett's, 'Twiggy in Her "One and Only" Phase', the *New York Times Magazine*, 10 May 1983.
41. 'Welcome Twiggy Mai Cosi' Moderna', Italian *Vogue*, April 1993.
42. 'This Little Twiggy', *Tatler*, September 1993.
43. Nick Knight for British *Vogue*, December 1999; Annie Leibovitz for American *Vogue*, November 1999.

PICTURE CREDITS

Every effort has been made to contact copyright holders; any omissions are inadvertent, and will be corrected in future editions if notification is given to the publisher in writing. We are grateful to the owners and lenders to the display and the following copyright holders who have kindly agreed to make their images available in this book.

PORTRAITS

p. 26: Photograph Ronald Traeger © Tessa Traeger/*Vogue*; pp. 29, 30: © Barry Lategan; p. 33 Barry Lategan/*Vogue* © The Condé Nast Publications Ltd; pp. 34, 35: © photograph by Allan Ballard; pp. 37, 38: © Photograph David Steen; p. 41:Twiggy, 1967, Bert Stern © Courtesy of Staley-Wise Gallery, New York; p. 42: *Twiggy, Paris, Vogue, 1967*, Bert Stern © Courtesy of Staley-Wise Gallery, New York; pp. 45, 46, 47, 48, 49, 51: Melvin Sokolsky © 2008; p. 52: *Richard Avedon with Twiggy, Paris studio, April 1967*. Photograph Richard Avedon © 2009 The Richard Avedon Foundation. Twiggy's Private Collection; p. 55: *Twiggy, dress by Robert Rojas, New York, April 1967*. Photograph Richard Avedon © 2009 The Richard Avedon Foundation; pp. 56–7: *Twiggy, hair by Ara Gallant, Paris, February 1968*. Photograph Richard Avedon © 2009 The Richard Avedon Foundation; p. 58: *Twiggy, diamond by Harry Winston, hair by Ara Gallant, September 1967*. Photograph Richard Avedon © 2009 The Richard Avedon Foundation; pp. 60, 61: Images reproduced in this book kindly made available through the generosity of the Scavullo Foundation; pp. 62, 63: © Estate of Jeanloup Sieff/*Vogue*; pp. 64: Photograph Ronald Traeger © Tessa Traeger. Collection National Portrait Gallery, London. NPG x125452; pp. 65, 69: Photograph Ronald Traeger © Tessa Traeger; pp. 66, 67: Photograph Ronald Traeger © Tessa Traeger/*Vogue*; p. 70: Cecil Beaton/*Vogue* © The Condé Nast Publications Ltd; p. 71: © Cecil Beaton Studio Archive, Sotheby's, London. Collection National Portrait Gallery, London. NPG x14224; pp. 72, 73: © Justin de Villeneuve. Twiggy's Private Collection; pp. 74–5: © Justin de Villeneuve. © Klaus Voormann; p. 76 © 1969 Paul McCartney. Photograph: Linda McCartney; pp. 79, 80, 81: Douglas Kirkland; pp. 83, 84: Courtesy Norman Parkinson Archive; p. 87: Terry O'Neill/Getty Images; pp. 88, 90–1, 93: © Steven Meisel/Art + Commerce; p. 94: © John Swannell. Twiggy's Private Collection; pp. 96, 97, 98–9: www.brianaris.com; p. 100: © Mary McCartney; pp. 102–3: © Annie Leibovitz/Contact Press Images, originally photographed for *Vogue*; p. 104: © Bryan Adams; p. 107: Mike Owen represented by www.models1creative.com; pp. 108, 109: © Sølve Sundsbø/Art + Commerce

CHRONOLOGY

All works are from Twiggy's Private Collection unless otherwise stated.

p. 110 Barry Lategan/*Tatler* © The Condé Nast Publications Ltd. Fig. 5: Photo © Lewis Morley Archive/National Portrait Gallery, London. RN 45827. Published in *London Life*; figs. 6, 7: © Barry Lategan; fig. 8: Terence Donovan/*Elle/Scoop*. The Twiggy Archive Loan Collection; fig. 9: © IPC + Syndication. Photograph Peter Carapetian. The Twiggy Archive Loan Collection; fig. 10: *Twiggy – Her Mod Mod Teen World* published by Beauty Secrets, Inc. The Twiggy Archive Loan Collection; fig. 11: *Twiggy, The Girl, The Look, The Scene* published by Atlas Magazines, Inc. Cover photograph Globe Photos. The Twiggy Archive Loan Collection; fig. 12: © Photograph by Allan Ballard. *Twiggy, The Girl, The Look, The Scene* published by Atlas Magazines, Inc. The Twiggy Archive Loan Collection; fig. 13: Central Press/Getty Images. The Twiggy Archive Loan Collection; fig. 14: Photograph Ronald Traeger © Tessa Traeger; fig. 15: Twiggy doll courtesy of Mattel, Inc. The Twiggy Archive Loan Collection; fig. 16: *Newsweek*, 4/10 © 1967. All rights reserved. Used by permission and protected by the Copyright Laws of the United States. The printing, copying, redistribution, or retransmission of

the Material without express written permission is prohibited. Photograph by Bert Stern. The Twiggy Archive Loan Collection; fig. 17: Topfoto. The Twiggy Archive Loan Collection; fig. 18: Marc Hispard/*Elle/Scoop*. The Twiggy Archive Loan Collection; fig. 19: June 1967 *Ladies' Home Journal*®. Photographs by Melvin Sokolsky; used with the permission from Meredith Corporation. The Twiggy Archive Loan Collection; fig. 20: *Seventeen* published by Hearst Communications, Inc. Photograph Carmen Schiavone. The Twiggy Loan Archive Collection; fig. 21: August 1967, Richard Avedon/*Vogue* © Condé Nast Publications. The Twiggy Loan Archive Collection; fig. 22: Photograph © Barry Lategan. *Look of London* published by Trixways Ltd. The Twiggy Archive Loan Collection; fig. 23: © Photograph David Steen. Published by Hawthorn Books (USA). The Twiggy Archive Loan Collection; fig. 24: Wesley/Getty Images. The Twiggy Archive Loan Collection; figs 25, 26: Photograph André Berg. *Mlle Age Tendre* published by Filipacchi – L'Union des Édition Modernes. The Twiggy Archive Loan Collection; figs 27, 28: © Justin de Villeneuve. *Queen* published by Stevens Press Ltd. The Twiggy Archive Loan Collection; fig. 29 © Justin de Villeneuve. *Hayat* Magazine. The Twiggy Archive Loan Collection; fig. 30 Fox Photos/Getty Images. The Twiggy Archive Loan Collection; fig. 31 © Justin de Villeneuve. Twiggy's Private Collection; figs 33, 34: Douglas Kirkland; fig. 35: 'The Boy Friend' © Turner Entertainment Co. A Warner Bros. Entertainment Company. All Rights Reserved. Twiggy's Private Collection; fig. 36: *The Australian Women's Weekly*, 7 July 1971. ACP Magazines. The Twiggy Archive Loan Collection; fig. 37: 'The Boy Friend' © Turner Entertainment Co. A Warner Bros. Entertainment Company. All Rights Reserved. The Twiggy Archive Loan Collection; fig. 39: © Justin de Villeneuve; fig. 41: Barry Lategan/*Vogue* © The Condé Nast Publications Ltd; fig. 42: Justin de Villeneuve/*Vogue* © The Condé Nast Publications Ltd; fig. 43: Album Cover Photograph by Justin de Villeneuve, Copyright Justin de Villeneuve. Makeup by Pierre Laroche. Lettering by Ray Campbell. Album Cover Courtesy of RZO Music © 1973/1997. Twiggy's Private Collection; fig. 45: Photograph © Justin de Villeneuve. Published by Hansom Books (UK) 1974. The Twiggy Archive Loan Collection; fig. 46: Front cover photograph © Justin de Villeneuve; back cover photograph © Barry Lategan. Published by Hart-Davis, MacGibbon (London). The Twiggy Archive Loan Collection; figs. 49, 51: These images appear courtesy of Mercury Records Limited. Photograph © Justin de Villeneuve. The Twiggy Archive Loan Collection; fig. 50: This image appears courtesy of Mercury Records Limited. The Twiggy Archive Loan Collection; fig. 53: Courtesy of Universal Studios Licensing LLLP. The Twiggy Archive Loan Collection; fig. 56: *Interview* Magazine, March 1983 featuring Twiggy. Courtesy Interview Inc. The Twiggy Archive Loan Collection; fig. 67: Record sleeve from 'Feel Emotion' by Twiggy courtesy of Sony Music Entertainment UK Ltd. The Twiggy Archive Loan Collection; fig. 72 © Steven Meisel/Art + Commerce. Courtesy of *Vogue Italia*; fig. 73: © REUTERS/Kevin Lamarque; fig. 75: Photograph www.brianaris.com. Published by Simon & Schuster. The Twiggy Archive Loan Collection; figs 76, 86: www.brianaris.com; fig. 78: Photograph for the *Times Magazine*, by Brigitte Lacombe; fig. 79: © John Swannell; background portrait © Barry Lategan; figs 82, 84: Photograph William Garrett at Wink Management. Art direction Steve Sharp, Marks & Spencer; fig. 85: Photograph www.brianaris.com. Published by Penguin/Michael Joseph. The Twiggy Archive Loan Collection; fig. 88: Image courtesy *i-D* magazine. March 2009. Photograph Sølve Sundsbø; fig. 89: supplied by Ketchum/Olay. Photographer Karan Kapoor

ACKNOWLEDGEMENTS

For their help in making this book, I should like to thank all the photographers whose work appears here and the administrators of their archives.

I am truly grateful to my agent Caroline Michel at Peters Fraser Dunlop, without whom this would never have happened.

It has been a great pleasure and privilege to work with the National Portrait Gallery, London. My special thanks go to Terence Pepper, Curator of Photographs, for working closely with me on the project. I would also like to thank Sandy Nairne, Director, and his wonderful colleagues, in particular the Photographs, Exhibitions and Events departments: Inga Fraser; Flora Fricker; Amy Guthrie; Sorcha Kennedy; Helen Trompeteler; and Ingrid Weiss.

Celia Joicey, Head of Publications, commissioned the book for the Gallery, and it was great fun working at such speed with her exceptional team, especially Christopher Tinker, Tamsin Perrett and Ruth Müller-Wirth. Lucy Macmillan has been a tireless and dedicated picture researcher, and I am grateful to John Edwards, who made the digital captures, and Patricia Burgess for proofreading.

In addition my thanks go to: Robin Muir, for his essay; Mike Dempsey and his team – Stephanie Jerey and Henrietta Molinaro – for the elegant design; and to James Parfitt, Gary Morris and the printer Westerham Press for their work.

The press and PR for the project has been expertly coordinated by Pallavi Vadhia and Eleanor Macnair at the National Portrait Gallery, with assistance from Mark Hutchinson and Hannah Blake at Colman Getty, my thanks also to them.

I am grateful to Sacha Walker, our PA, for her conscientious work.

My thanks to Carly and Ace, for their love and support.

Finally, extra special thanks to Leigh Lawson, for helping me to write the text, co-ordinating the project and always being there for me.